DEALS AND DOLLARS

AUTHORED BY WILLIAM OCHIENG

DEALS AND DOLLARS

(The Ultimate Guide to Business Success)

by William O. Ochieng.

DEALS AND DOLLARS

Copyright © 2020 by William Omondi Ochieng.

All rights reserved. This book is protected under the copyright laws of the Republic of Kenya. No part of this publication may be reproduced, distributed, stored in a retrieval system or transmitted in any form or by any means, including electronic, mechanical, photocopying, recording or otherwise without the prior written permission of the publisher, except in the case of brief quotations embodied in critical reviews and certain other non-commercial uses permitted by copyright law.

For permission requests, write to the publisher, addressed:

"Attention: Permission to Use" at the address below.

WILLIAM OMONDI OCHIENG,

42155-00100 GPO,

NAIROBI

Email address:

williamochieng.author@gmail.com or williamochieng.business@gmail.com

Any references to historic events, real people, or real places are purely coincidental. Names, characters and places are products of the author's imagination. The story is inspired by true events however, certain scenes, dialogue, events and occurrences have been altered for dramatic purposes.

Front cover page by Mr. Emmanuel Otieno of E-Productions.

Book design by Mr. Emmanuel Otieno of E-Productions.

Editing by Miss. Joyce Akoth.

Printed by Amazon.

First printing edition 2020.

AUTHORED BY WILLIAM OCHIENG

TABLE OF CONTENTS

TABLE OF CONTENTS IV

DEDICATION VI

PREFACE VII

INTRODUCTION IX

PART I: MINDSET 1

MENTAL PREPARATION 1

CHAPTER 1: WHO? 2

CHAPTER 2: WHY? 5

CHAPTER 3: HOW? 7

CHAPTER 4: WHERE? 10

CHAPTER 1: IT IS TIME 12

CHAPTER 2: THINK THINGS THROUGH 14

CHAPTER 3: PUT IT DOWN ON PAPER 16

CHAPTER 4: DO RESEARCH 19

CHAPTER 5: TAKE TIME TO CONSOLIDATE 21

PART III: TIME TO EXECUTE...24

DEALS AND DOLLARS

CHAPTER 1: PUT THE PLAN INTO ACTION 24

CHAPTER 2: BUILD A TEAM 27

CHAPTER 3: BUILD THE INFRASTRUCTURE 31

CHAPTER 4: INVEST IN MARKETING 33

CHAPTER 5: OPEN DOORS TO CUSTOMERS 35

PART IV: WALK OUTSIDE THE FENCE 38

CHAPTER 1: OBSERVE 38

CHAPTER 2: MAKE CHANGES 40

CHAPTER 3: OBSERVE AGAIN 43

CHAPTER 4: SCRAP IT OR AMPLIFY IT 46

PART V: CONGRATULATIONS, NOW WHAT? 50

CHAPTER 1: CONCLUSION 50

ABOUT THE AUTHOR 53

AUTHORED BY WILLIAM OCHIENG

DEDICATION

This book is dedicated to the almighty God as well as my family which includes: My father James Ochieng Isanda, my mother Beatrice Mwende Kilonzo, my sister Joyce Akoth Ochieng and my brother Emmanuel Otieno Ochieng.

"FAMILY IS POWER." – WILLIAM O. OCHIENG

PREFACE

I wrote this book to serve as a guide for attaining the highest possible level of success in entrepreneurship. The book contains content compiled from motivational speeches I delivered, both formally and informally, to business leaders as well as aspiring entrepreneurs over a period of three (3) years.

Many people have great ideas which have the potential to change the world but they lack knowledge of how to go about it. **"DEALS AND DOLLARS"** is intended to bridge this gap by equipping its readers with all they need to know about starting and running a successful business.

The book walks its readers through a step by step process that will ultimately result in the establishment of a profitable venture.

A burning desire to inspire greatness in you is what highly motivated me during the entire process of developing and writing this book. I am aiming at helping you, the reader, to recognize that you already have what it takes to become a successful entrepreneur. It can be done.

This book is intended for all types of audience and that is why features like the use of basic English language have been employed. As an author, I believe that you are special and that deep down within you is the ability to change the world positively.

AUTHORED BY WILLIAM OCHIENG

This is the right time for you and I to awaken the beast inside, dream big ideas, develop workable implementation plans and see them to fruition.

Greatness can be achieved from small beginnings.

Mr. William O. Ochieng,
Author and Entrepreneur.

INTRODUCTION

"All men dream, but not equally. Those who dream by night in the dusty recesses of their minds wake in the day to find that it was vanity, but the dreamers of the day are dangerous men, for they may act their dream with open eyes to make it possible. This I did."

T.E. Lawrence
"Lawrence of Arabia"

PART I: MINDSET

"GIVE A MAN A FISH AND YOU FEED HIM FOR A DAY. TEACH A MAN TO FISH AND YOU FEED HIM FOR A LIFETIME."

– SAYGIN YALCIN.

MENTAL PREPARATION

First and foremost, before you think about starting a business and making money, you need to get some few things in order. "Okay, so what are these things?" you might ask. Well, let me tell you that they are some of the most important stuff you will ever think about.

Reason is that before you start contemplating about the business, you have to ask yourself four very important questions that are fundamental to the success of the venture. Unless you are planning to fail in business, it is of paramount importance that you consider these four lines of thought that will help you organize yourself better and prepare for all that is to come.

Let us explore these things in detail.

CHAPTER 1: WHO?

Who are you? This is the first question you should ask yourself before thinking about anything else. Understanding yourself helps in eliminating any doubts that may arise in future concerning whether the venture was the right thing for you or not. It is of no value to anyone if you start second guessing yourself in future and questioning your every decision. As an entrepreneur, you need to be sure of who you are. You need to own your existence and have an absolute belief that you are capable of delivering the best product to your customers.

You will not do this without understanding yourself. Your body, mind and soul need to be in harmony with each other. Your mind and your heart need to communicate to each other as well as trust the feeling that each has.

Of course, self-awareness can be achieved through stuff like yoga, meditation etc. but today, I want to give you a simpler way to achieve self-awareness without having to pay someone. My method is this;

Take some time off your daily routine, around four days should do the trick. During these four days, do not engage in anything related in any way whatsoever to what it is you do during other days.

DEALS AND DOLLARS

For example, if you are a professional boxer, then take some time away from the gym. If you are an accountant then take some time away from the office etc. The point is do something totally different with your life and then after the four days are over, go to a quiet place, preferably a safe space, a place where you always feel the most comfortable to be alone and free to think. Then, ask yourself this, "What are my top 10 strengths?" and then ask yourself, "what are my top 10 weaknesses?"

Use your fingers to count them down. Take as much time as possible and do not rush the process at all. Doing this simple activity bears some significant importance. By engaging in it, you will become more self-aware.

The four day off period is a strategic process aimed at psychologically opening your mind to some of the deepest sentiments buried in the subconscious. The using of fingers to count down your thoughts does not only function to pull the sentiments from the subconscious and bring them into the conscious but it also helps to commit them into memory.

That is why I prefer using that method instead of the conventional pen and paper one. With a notebook, you are bound to forget about the ten (10) strengths and ten (10) weaknesses because your brain knows that you wrote them down therefore, when there is need to remember them you will revisit the notebook.

By counting them down using your fingers, the brain knows that without writing them somewhere, the only option of remembering them is by committing the ideas to memory. Here, you stand a better chance of recollecting events when the time comes to do so.

By knowing your strengths and weaknesses, you will achieve a self-awareness level that passes the threshold required to be an entrepreneur. Here you clearly know what is good for you and what is not. Now the only thing left to watch out for is ignorance because in as much as you have achieved a higher self-awareness level, you can easily ignore valuable warning signs that may lead you to engage in business that exposes your weaknesses.

Whenever you feel like there is a temptation to double-back on old habits that you may have resolved to stay away from, always remember this process, take some time off, figure out your strengths and weaknesses, then stay away from your weaknesses.

The secret to defeating your weaknesses is learning about your strengths. Always keep that in mind.

CHAPTER 2: WHY?

After getting a clear understanding of who you are and what you are capable of doing, you have to ask yourself another big question which is "Why?".

Specifically,

1. Why do you want to start a business?
2. Why did you decide to do it now?
3. Why not stay employed at your workplace?
4. Why your business idea?
5. Why the risk and can you afford the risk?
6. Why you?

These questions will give you a better understanding of the reason behind whatever is driving you. They are a key to knowing the type of energy that is fueling your driving force, your motivation. By the way this is very important to understand because through engaging in this process, you will comprehend the level of seriousness behind your prospective decision as well as how much are you willing to put on the line for it at any given day or time.

Skipping this process is what leads to some entrepreneurs closing down their businesses when the going gets tough. Honestly, it is not their fault because they were just exploring the option of having their own business.

The only problem is that in business, there is no room for experiments. You either know why you are doing it or you don't. To put it plainly, you can't eat your cake and have it too.

You need to be sure of what you are doing at all times and confident that the benefits will always outweigh the cost. Successful entrepreneurs are not ordinary gamblers but are calculated gamblers. You need to know exactly what you are doing, why you are doing it and the risks involved.

All these are things you can do yourself because I have some good news for you. This news is that no one on earth knows you better that yourself. Just take time and think things through all by yourself.

Of course, you can ask for advice from friends and relatives but in the end remember that whatever they are telling you are only opinions. You and only you have the power to make the final decision.

CHAPTER 3: HOW?

After figuring out who you are and also why you want to be in business, you have to now sit down and think about how you are going to achieve your objectives. Now, at this point in time, you should not have any doubts about yourself at all. All your strengths and weaknesses should be fully known to you. Your reasons for engaging in business should also be copiously known to you. There should be no gaps regarding those queries and if there are, then you should not proceed with this guide until those gaps are filled to the brim.

Reason is that in this step, you are going to engage in a very complex process that requires complete self-realization. If you have not fully realized yourself as a person then you will never move past this stage. People will question your ideas and with every question that you cannot answer there will be significant damage to your morale which will eventually lead to you forfeiting the business idea completely.

AUTHORED BY WILLIAM OCHIENG

An individual who has fully identified his/her strengths and weaknesses; and has also understood why he/she needs to engage in the business will never succumb to the doubts and discouragements raised by friends and relatives. The worst damage he/she will take is general discouragement but this will not deter him/her from forging on against all odds to make his/her dreams come true.

In the same way that you can take a book from a person's hand but you cannot take the knowledge of what the person read is actually the same as what happens in this scenario. People in your life will discourage you, voice concerns and discouragement comments. It is judicious to listen to them and take what people say into advisement but for someone who is not fully realized, he/she will succumb to the opinions of others and give up hope. However, a person who has fully realized himself/ herself will be in a much better position to resist the temptation to give up on his/her dream.

The question of how can be answered through developing a plan. This plan should be a rough idea of what you hope to accomplish, how you expect to accomplish them and the chronological order of the objectives.

DEALS AND DOLLARS

Here, most people go overboard by developing strategic plans and budget forecasts. Please do not follow that trend because there is no need for that here. All you need to know and have is a rough mental pictographic concept of how you will go about executing your business idea.

Don't get me wrong, strategic plans, budget forecasts and business plans are all good things because we know that failing to plan is planning to fail. We will even talk about them in future but they are not relevant to us here. At this stage, just take a pen and paper then write down how you expect to achieve your objectives in a way that you understand.

You don't have to follow some international standards set somewhere. All you need is within you. Let your imagination go wild. Allow yourself to dream. It is free of charge, fun and also healthy. Do a draft of what you want to do and how you want to do it.

It is that simple. The only important thing is that in the end please make sure that you clearly understand everything you wrote and there is nothing else left lurking in the dusty recesses of your mind. Put everything down on paper.

AUTHORED BY WILLIAM OCHIENG

CHAPTER 4: WHERE?

Finally, let us explore the question of where. This is a question that can only be answered after the other three questions have been answered. By where I simply mean the location of the business venture.

This is an important question to ask because any business needs a physical location where employees can meet once in a while (if it is an online business) and where customers can voice their concerns. A business has to have an office. This is even a requirement by legislation in some countries.

There are very many reasons as to why a business needs a physical location. I will not get into the fine print but just know that this is an area which deserves your time, energy and thought.

One factor that is usually buried in the fine print regarding location is convenience. I would like to expound on this factor abit because it is very important. So, in terms of convenience, you need to select a business location that is convenient. The factor of convenience should not only stretch and cover you as an entrepreneur but also the employees as well as customers. You also need to select a business location that is convenient to the business itself. What I mean is that it should be a place that enables you as the entrepreneur incur the cheapest cost while pooling together the factors of production.

DEALS AND DOLLARS

What are factors of production? Factors of production are land, capital, labour and entrepreneurship. In much simpler terms, these are the basic resources that enable business operations to take place.

It is the responsibility if an entrepreneur to pool together all the other factors of production and bring them into business. Therefore, all responsibilities relating to the factors of production such as capital are incurred by the entrepreneur. The entrepreneur may also reap rewards from these factors of production such as profit.

It is important for the entrepreneur to minimize the cost and maximize the profit of any business venture. This responsibility can be greatly influenced by the business location because think about this, it becomes more expensive to transport labour into the business if the premises are off the grid. It also becomes more expensive to transport raw materials into the business if the premises are off the grid.

As an entrepreneur you need to ensure that your business location is in your favour and not the other way around.

PART II: MAP OUT YOUR IDEAS

"EMBRACE DISCOMFORT. INNOVATION LIES BETWEEN A ROCK AND A HARD PLACE."

– JESSICA O. MATTHEWS.

CHAPTER 1: IT IS TIME

With your mindset now poised for success, it's now time to map out your ideas. Remember in the previous section we talked about writing down all your thoughts, ideas, goals, objectives and everything else in a chronological order. Well, it's now time to organize that data into something that meets international standards.

Doing this is important because in business it is inevitable that one day you will pitch your idea to someone. This someone can be an investor, lender, family friend or even your family. What you are aiming at is to have your thoughts organized in a fashion that every single one of these people will understand what you are talking about just after reading the documents you will have fashioned them with.

DEALS AND DOLLARS

This will not only save you time in pitching your ideas but will also boost your integrity by making people take you more seriously.

How you talk, walk, eat, sleep, work and even laugh are key non-verbal cues that either make or break your reputation as an entrepreneur. Being an entrepreneur is a full-time job. You are always on the spotlight. Anything you do will directly be associated with your business and there is nothing you can do about that.

Therefore, every single aspect of your professional life needs to be mapped out properly and professionally.

CHAPTER 2: THINK THINGS THROUGH

The first process here is to think things through. This sounds easy but believe me when I say that it is not. Your business will be a lifetime commitment. Everything you do from the moment you commence operations will be revolving around the business. Your habits, family, time and very many other factors will need to be adjusted. Your life will become your business and you need to think things through in order to figure out whether all these are risks you are willing to bear.

In entrepreneurship, passion beats profession. How much you love your business will determine by how far you are going to beat your competitors. By the way, I am not talking about the romantic type of love but the business type of love. The easiest way to determine by how much you love your business is to ask yourself, "How much invested are you in it?"

Think about this, we spend a lot of time doing things we love and we also enjoy the company of people we love. This same narrative applies in business in the sense that if you are the type of person who frowns or sighs whenever a topic that involves your business comes up then you clearly do not love your business and you should do something about it.

DEALS AND DOLLARS

A business should be like your fist love. It should be intense, beautiful, exciting and most importantly profitable.

You need to be sure that the business venture is for you and you are for the business venture. Once you commit to doing it then you are in it for life. Everything in your life will have to welcome the business as a new part of who you are as a person.

So, remember to think things through. Take even weeks to do this. Talk to everyone important in your life and do proper soul searching because after this stage there is no turning back.

A clear example of how serious this can be is seen where a couple decides to have a healthy child but, after birth the child is born with some very unusual features. The couple cannot order the hospital to kill the child and go home to try having another baby. They are required by law to take the child as he/she is or give him/her out but not kill the child.

The same concept can be applied to business. If things go south, and they often do, you cannot kill your business that easily because of very many factors. Some of these factors even include legislation and the capital invested in the business.

You will have to bear the brunt and hold on to the hope that things will get better.

AUTHORED BY WILLIAM OCHIENG

In order for you to even have the possibility of conceiving this hope, you need to have been sure of who you are and you also need to be very much in love with your business.

CHAPTER 3: PUT IT DOWN ON PAPER

After thinking things through, it is now time to put your business ideas on paper professionally. Here you will need some knowledge in Finance and Accounting but do not worry if you do not have this because, the beauty about being an entrepreneur is that you do not need to have every skill. All you need is the ability to pool resources and you are all set.

This applies here because you are going to secure the services of a professional in the finance or accounting industry. If you are one of them then well and good but if not then do not worry and hire someone, preferably a friend.

Reason why I am suggesting a friend or just someone close in general is because if you present your idea to someone who is untrustworthy, he/she may steal your beautiful idea and implement it somewhere else. Non-Disclosure Agreements (NDAs) will not help you here because there are a lot of loop holes when it comes to talking about ideas concerning an unregistered business entity.

DEALS AND DOLLARS

Do not get me wrong, Non-Disclosure Agreements (NDAs) are good but they are a luxury you cannot afford when it comes to a very high margin business idea like let's say a restaurant that cooks using a secret family recipe.

I know what you are thinking. A restaurant that cooks using a secret family recipe. Isn't that a reason that qualifies for a Non-Disclosure Agreements (NDAs)? Well, you are correct but in some countries in order to secure a Non-Disclosure Agreement (NDA) related to business ideas you need to disclose it to the attorney of record. Well, some countries have a track record of having attorneys violate the attorney-client privilege that is supposed to protect your idea. So, if you trust the legal system in your country then get a Non-Disclosure Agreement (NDA) but if you don't then do not dare. Keep the idea to yourself and do not disclose the inner secrets of the business to the finance or accounting professional you hire no matter how hard they press you for the information.

I can tell you beyond any reasonable doubt that a finance and an accounting professional can develop very accurate business models without knowing the family secret recipe in your business.

Some of the things you need to put down and develop include the following:
1. A Business Plan
2. A Business Proposal

3. A Business Model
4. A Master Budget
5. A Budgeted Income Statement
6. A Budgeted Statement of Financial Position (Balance Sheet)

All of the above are technical things that I will put up content about in another book. Here I just want you to understand how to go about starting and running a successful business. I also want you to learn some of the tricks that successful entrepreneurs may not want you to know.

With this in mind I do not want to overcomplicate this guide with a lot of technical content but if you need the technical aspect these things, I will make them available in other books.

For now, all you need to know is that the six (6) items mentioned above are a necessity for business success. They will enable you to answer any queries you may encounter along the way. To assist in developing the six (6) documents you will need to use the notebook where you wrote down the business idea itself. This will enable you to have all the information you need captured in these important six (6) documents.

DEALS AND DOLLARS

Remember to take your time, there is no need to rush things because what you are engaging in is among the foundations of the business. If the business has a faulty foundation then it is doomed to collapse eventually.

CHAPTER 4: DO RESEARCH

After having everything is noted down on paper, it is time to conduct a business research process. Here, you will use the six (6) documents to analyze the market thoroughly. You can engage a professional researcher in this process if you want to.

Things to look for at this stage include the following:
1. Where does your business fit in the market?
2. With your capital, how big can you start?
3. Who are your competitors in the market segment?
4. If the industry is welcoming to you?
5. If everything captured in the documents is applicable in reality?
6. How feasible is the business?

You can add other things to the checklist but the above questions should not miss out in your research. This research is intended to offer a clear picture of what to expect once you put the documents we have discussed in the previous section into action. How you go about this is entirely upto you. The important thing is that you are able to see how the world responds to your clearly mapped out ideas.

DEALS AND DOLLARS

During this stage, remember to always keep an open mind because you may learn something great that can be incorporated to your already developed business documents.

As you also conduct the research, remember to involve some professionals to act as consultants and advisors who will provide guidance on areas to examine depending on the type of business you are aspiring to start as well as the business model you have adopted.

The process is entirely yours but having these professionals as shadows will help in ensuring that you cover all bases that need to be covered.

You are having them there as a precaution so remember not to hire someone full-time unless you want to.

CHAPTER 5: TAKE TIME TO CONSOLIDATE

After finishing up on the research it is now time for the final process in mapping out your ideas. What you are now going to do is called consolidation of ideas. This is where you will wind up the entire process of mapping out your ideas.

Here you will take the business documents that you had developed earlier on or had a professional develop them for you, and you will compare notes with the ground business research you had conducted. The purpose for this is to try and find out whether the business documents are as accurate as possible.

The ground research may reveal information that you may not have previously known or even new additional information. It is of paramount importance that this new information is captured in the business documents.

An adjustment at this stage will definitely cost you far less that an adjustment made after the business is up and running. By the way it is important for me to point out that I am not giving out a strategy aimed at eliminating risk but rather a strategy aimed at abating risk. It is impossible to eliminate all the risk in a business venture therefore; it is the duty of the entrepreneur to minimize risk as much as possible to the best of his/her competence.

DEALS AND DOLLARS

This consolidation process ensures that no risk that was unearthed during the research process is left unaccounted for in the business documents. At this stage, you will develop the final business documents that are needed to guide your venture to success. These are just the updated documents of the:

1. Business Plan
2. Business Proposal
3. Business Model
4. Master Budget
5. Budgeted Income Statement
6. Budgeted Statement of Financial Position (Balance Sheet)

Remember that, updated documents are just the original documents adjusted for risk.

After developing these updated documents, you need to find an attorney who will notarize every single document that needs notarization. This will make your work ready and more appealing to lenders and other financial institutions.

AUTHORED BY WILLIAM OCHIENG

Remember as an entrepreneur, people see you as the business you are running. The venture becomes an automatic part of your identity therefore, it is important that you present yourself as a serious person who is organized, respectful, trustworthy, humble, focused and extremely time conscious. These are just but afew of the characteristics of a good entrepreneur.

As you can guess, I have given you only the most relevant ones in the real business world.

PART III: TIME TO EXECUTE

"DON'T WORRY ABOUT FAILURE; YOU ONLY HAVE TO BE RIGHT ONCE."

– DREW HOUSTON.

CHAPTER 1: PUT THE PLAN INTO ACTION

You have done all the preparation work and now it is time to execute the plan developed. Most people say that this is the most difficult part of establishing a business but I personally beg to differ.

Reason is that the hardest part was developing a workable plan for executing the business itself. The entrepreneurs who find it difficult to stablish a business are the ones who did not see the need to develop a feasible plan before hitting the ground. As I said earlier in a previous chapter, failing to plan is planning to fail.

The business documents that you have developed act as a compass and road map in your quest of navigating the business world. Without your compass and road map then you are definitely doomed to get lost in the business world.

AUTHORED BY WILLIAM OCHIENG

The business documents you developed will work for you here. All you need is to follow the processes and steps highlighted in the documents. If it is your first time in establishing a business or you feel like you lack the knowledge and expertise to go about the first few stages then do not worry. You only need to secure the services of a professional once again. Either an Attorney, an Accountant or any other professional you desire will be of assistance to you.

All you or the professional acting on your behalf need to do is to oversee the proper registration of your business. This is coupled by establishing the infrastructure needed at the business location.

There will be nothing new you are doing at this point but just following the plan you had originally developed.

After registering the business and establishing all the infrastructure needed at the business location you are almost ready for your customers. The key point here is you are almost ready.

One of the most common mistakes entrepreneurs commit is rushing things.

They get too much excited about making money to an extent where they mess up during these final crucial stages.

DEALS AND DOLLARS

Most of the time business registration takes time. This also depends on the type of business you are establishing. While the authority responsible for registering the business is working on it, you can use the wait time to build some other crucial components of the business infrastructure.

CHAPTER 2: BUILD A TEAM

Now, this is one of the areas where you seriously need to devote some time into because we are now going to discuss a matter that literally determines the life or death for your company. I need you to be extra attentive on this part. A team should be an extension of yourself as the business owner. Do not listen to the noise in the industry that may steer you from this argument.

Many experts out there will tell you to take people as they are. They will say that you should not judge people's actions, characters or even past history in terms of track record. Well, I agree with them when it comes to everyday life but when it comes to business, I tend to strongly disagree with them.

Reason is as I have mentioned above, a team is an extension of yourself as the business owner. It is like another limb in your body.

Just like a limb in your body, you need to have a team that is reliable, trustworthy, predictable, dependable and fully qualified for the job. If you disagree with this then think about this for a second. When you wake up in the morning, do you assume or do you know that your body parts are just the way you left them when you slept at night.

In most cases you know.

DEALS AND DOLLARS

When you want to ask a question, do you assume or do you know that your hand is going to shoot up straight in the air?

In most cases you know.

When your brain comes up with a nice story that you would like to share with your friends, do you assume or do you know that your mouth is going to say the words you want to say?

Guess what, in most cases you know.

In the same way you trust your body to do what you want it to do, you should also be capable of according that same level of trust to your team.

You need to have a team in place that does exactly what you want even before you think about it. You need to have a team that follows your instructions and always asks you for permission before making amendments to your directives. You need to have a team that is qualified and competent enough to run your business without your physical presence.

They need to be an extension of yourself.

Now, if your business is a multi-million-dollar corporation then you do not need to worry about this so much because there are a lot of dynamics that go into selecting your team.

However, if your business is a start-up and by that, I mean that it is less than five (5) years old then you seriously need to take my advice into consideration. Reason here is that for a start-up, there are going to be quite a lot of unforeseen bad situations. Without a solid team that passes my selection criteria, you are bound to become stressed to a point where you even quit your business.

I have seen it happen to some entrepreneurs. I have also seen other entrepreneurs who are the Chief Executive Officers (CEOs) of their start-up firms being kicked out of their businesses by their Boards of Management just because the business idea was too sweet and the team wanted total control over it, even if it meant kicking out the person who came up with the idea in the first place.

So be careful. Allocate enough time to selecting your team. Follow all the guidelines set by regulatory institutions but also remember that the team is an extension of yourself. Just like the way the body can reject a transplanted organ reminisce that you also have the power to reject people who will slow down your success.

As a business owner you need to have the least amount of stress from internal operations of your business. This will allow you to focus more on the external mechanics like securing more clients and searching for cheaper suppliers. By the way, external mechanics of your business are of supreme importance during the start-up period.

DEALS AND DOLLARS

You need to solidify your position in the market as fast as possible. This will not only reel in more clients but it will boost other financial metrics like cashflows which financial institutions like banks look at when determining your credit worthiness. You will have an easier time convincing lenders and investors to invest in your business when your financial records are of superior quality and of seriously great health.

Remember that the clock starts the moment your business is registered. Financial analysts analyze data from that point henceforth so, prove to the world that your business is a hot cake by showing productivity in the first early years.

CHAPTER 3: BUILD THE INFRASTRUCTURE

Now that you have a team it is time to build an infrastructure for your business. By infrastructure I am not talking about roads, railway lines etc. unless your business involves them.

I am talking about the necessary equipment that will enable you produce the necessary goods and services you intend to sell to your customers. These include plant, machinery, buildings, office equipment and even business vehicles.

By carefully following the plans initially developed for your business, you will be able to execute informed decisions when setting up everything needed. All you need to watch out for in this area is conmen and suppliers who deliver goods that are below standard.

As an entrepreneur try to learn as much about prices of different products needed in your business. This will give you an edge later when reading through the different cost analysis statements developed by your cost accountants. It will also minimize the chances of fraudulent practices.

If possible, involve some experts in this stage but only if your budget allows it. Remember not to spend on things you do not need. Bleeding cash out of your business is not something you want to tolerate at all as a business owner.

DEALS AND DOLLARS

Some of the experts you need to involve include formal organization experts, business consultants as well as procurement and supply chain experts. You can also include some market experts to advise on pricing matters.

If you are procuring expensive assets which are either fixed or current assets then be sure to conduct proper asset valuation. Here you can involve highly qualified asset valuers who are of course within your budget.

While building your infrastructure always remember to keep an open mind. This is important because there is always a possibility you may come across something better than what you hoped for or even something worse. Keeping an open mind will allow you to safely navigate through this stage but always keep the developed business plans close to your heart.

CHAPTER 4: INVEST IN MARKETING

Now that you have a solid team and the best infrastructure available you can now venture into marketing. A lot of people have the mentality that marketing is something very difficult. Some even say that it should only be left to celebrities and social media influencers but today I am here to tell you that you can do it.

"How?" you may ask. Well, you do not have to become a celebrity or a social media influencer but you can most definitely use them. Remember that they are doing it for money and in your budget, you have some cash budgeted for marketing. Use that money to pay them for their services but do not make the mistake that everyone does which is dealing with them directly.

Be smart and use a cut-out. In this case your cut-out will be a marketing consultant. Find someone within your budget and work with them to advertise your business. Using a marketing consultant as a cut-out is very beneficial. One of these benefits is that he/she will work with the celebrities and social media influencers in his/her network to boost your presence in the world. This will save you a lot of time and effort in not only finding these people but striking a practical deal with them.

DEALS AND DOLLARS

In entrepreneurship, you need to let things work for you as much as possible. Just make the deal and the dollars will come later. Always remember that you are an entrepreneur and not self-employed.

You are the boss.

CHAPTER 5: OPEN DOORS TO CUSTOMERS

Immediately marketing starts you are going to start getting traffic. There will be a lot of questions about your business coming left, right and centre.

What you need to do at the point traffic starts flowing is set-up an opening day or a business launch day. This will be the day you fully open the doors of your business to members of the public. By this day, you should have everything up and running at one hundred percent (100%).

Before the D-day, allow customers to pre-order your goods or services. Do not sell but allow them to pre-order. The mistake most entrepreneurs make is that they start selling their products as soon as the first one is ready to be sold. This is of course not bad at all but here they greatly risk their reputation. Reason is that an unsatisfied customer will quickly spread word that your business is bad and this will drive away any prospective customers you had.

By setting a launch date and collecting orders before the day (pre-orders) you are saving yourself the risk of damaging your reputation in case your products do not meet the expectations of your customers.

DEALS AND DOLLARS

You are also making it easy logistically to gather the bio data of your fist customers, the day sale was made, any feedback they have (both positive and negative) and also the numbers (customers, sales and margins). Conducting first sale at the launch date will enable you to make workable plans to adjust production as well as service delivery of your products. You are also making it easier for the research and development team to quickly understand the needs as well as the expectations of your customers. They will be able to develop accurate intervention strategies faster than when they receive data in small bits progressively.

A launch date also announces to the world that you are a serious player in the game. It is a show of force tactic. People who would not have initially considered being your customers will be attracted to your business when they hear about a colourful launch somewhere that is either online or at a physical location. It also shows investors that you are organized and serious about your business.

Hit the ground with the largest bang you can because it will transpire into sales. If possible, also run a promotional week where you offer your products at a discounted price. This is aimed at driving more traffic into your business. Give your business all you can during the first few weeks and months since inception. If you fail to prove to the world that you exist then no one will recognize you and this means that you will have low or even zero (0) sales.

AUTHORED BY WILLIAM OCHIENG

Make a good impression on the market. Show you that you have arrived strong and you are running the best business in existence. Drown your competitors in your glory and always remember that small things in entrepreneurship make perfection, but perfection itself is no small thing.

PART IV: WALK OUTSIDE THE FENCE

"YOUR MOST UNHAPPY CUSTOMERS ARE YOUR GREATEST SOURCE OF LEARNING."

– BILL GATES.

CHAPTER 1: OBSERVE

After establishing your business, do not waste time enforcing new changes all the time. Reason is that as a business commences its operations, there are bound to be some hick-ups that you may not have foreseen.

Sometimes the entire market may change and be against all the plans you had initially developed. Let this not deter you and force you into making rash decisions. Take some time and walk outside the fence.

AUTHORED BY WILLIAM OCHIENG

By this, I mean that you should imagine yourself fenced out of your business for some time. Do nothing major but observe. Just observe. Look at how the different business operations are being done, look at how your employees work, study the culture of your business, learn the consumer behaviour of your business and also try to identify the key things that define your business (things that when removed from the equation will cause the death of your business).

It is important to understand these things because the secret to running a successful business is knowing your business. Knowing what happens in every department will give you an edge in making better counter decisions.

Of course, by observing I do not mean that you should not work or execute your daily duties. All I am saying is that you need to observe more than how you react to situations. Learn as much as you can about everything.

To help you in this process, you can procure professional services from financial and business analysts. They will be able to assist in making proper identification of root problems that may hinder the business success in future.

The advantage of using these professionals is that they will not only do the physical observing but the financial type of observing which involves conducting a proper analysis of the business records. These records include everything from books of account to the various plans developed earlier in the business. The professionals may also conduct a variance analysis that will enable them to determine by how far the business has deviated from the plans originally developed.

Please understand that there are very many ways of conducting the observation process. If I discuss all of them in detail then this book would become intensely boring. As an entrepreneur you are allowed to be creative. It is legal to think outside the box and sometimes to even ignore if there is even a box present.

CHAPTER 2: MAKE CHANGES

After conducting a careful observation process, it is now time to implement the necessary changes (if any) that serve as a corrective measure to observed problems. Implementing these changes is much harder than it seems because established systems and even people have a natural tendency to resist change.

As a result of this, you need to be very careful while undergoing this process. There is little room available for errors therefore, you need spot on precision. In order to achieve this level of precision, you can make use of experts or specialists in planning as well as enforcement of certain directives. Most of these professionals operate as consultants.

From them, you need a workable execution strategy to be developed. Just give them the observation points you had gathered and then allow them ample time to craft a workable plan. After they have done so, take some time to review their work, ask questions in order to get clarification and even send them back to the drawing board if their suggestions aren't satisfactory enough.

Remember that you are the boss and only what you say goes. Whatever anyone else tells you are just opinions but your word is the decision.

I felt the importance to mention this because there are entrepreneurs who become so dependent of consultants to an extent where they accord the consultants power over them.

These consultants end up taking advantage of the weak-minded entrepreneur by adopting an indirect governance over the business of the entrepreneur. I have seen this happen and sometimes the consultants even conduct hostile takeovers on their client's business.

DEALS AND DOLLARS

In simple terms, a hostile takeover involves going directly to the board members or shareholders of a particular company or business and initiating a process to buy or change ownership of the entire business from the current owner most likely without his/her knowledge.

Never forget that you are the boss of your business. So, think and act like one.

After deliberations with the consultants or even the respective business experts you have engaged, it is time to implement the plan. A solid plan rarely encounters serious challenges during implementation. Reason is that most of the expected problems will have been accounted for in advance and corrective measures put in place.

During implementation, remember to keep a calm and cool mind. Your employees have the ability to read through you. Confidence in you spikes confidence in each one of them. Indecisiveness in you spikes fear in each one of them.

You are the key to their individual moods so please make a positive contribution.

CHAPTER 3: OBSERVE AGAIN

The plan is in force, the corrective measures are now taking into effect. There is nothing left to do right? But no, you are wrong because as an entrepreneur, you have to make sure that everything is going smoothly. The only way you can do this is by conducting another observation run.

Just like you did in the first round, you will conduct the process all over again. The only difference this time is that you already have the first run to serve as a benchmark and the plan enforced thereafter to serve as a point of reference.

Some of the main things to watch out for include the state of mind of your employees, the adaptability level of the customers to the changes, the different margins like profit and also the level of expenses.

It is important to track these key data points during this second observation run. You also have the freedom to add any other metrics that you deem necessary as per your own opinion or that of your business advisors.

Keep a close eye on every aspect of the business; both financial and social.

DEALS AND DOLLARS

Most entrepreneurs make the mistake of ignoring the social factors revolving around their business. These include the level of happiness of their employees, the satisfaction level of their customers and even the confidence level of their investors.

They only focus on the financial factors which are things like profit/loss, expenses or even sales. This is by no means wrong but as an entrepreneur you need to develop a wholistic approach when it comes to running a business. By this I mean that you need to be invested in the Legal department just as much as you are invested in the Human Resources department or the Information Technology department.

Adopt a bird's eye view of the business and this will help you in making better decisions that are well informed. One thing that causes entrepreneurs to play favourites in their businesses is their individual professional experience or career. For example, an entrepreneur who is an accountant by profession may sub consciously invest too much time into the Accounts department of his/her business. This is by no means horrible but you need to constantly remind yourself that you are not an employee of the Accounts department but the entire business. You have a much bigger role to play and a set of very different rules to play by. You need to think about everyone working for you and not just the accountants whom you can relate to careerwise.

AUTHORED BY WILLIAM OCHIENG

(Please note that I have used accountants as an example for my point. Any professional career has equal potential to deviate the focus of the entrepreneur thus lead him/her to play favourites)

Ensure that all the changes you wanted to make are properly incorporated into the business. Also ensure that the voices of all the stakeholders in your business are heard as loudly and clearly as possible.

Remember that you have a team that is readily available for you to work with. You do not answer to them but always make them feel important and appreciated. Listen to them as much as possible and treat them as human beings.

CHAPTER 4: SCRAP IT OR AMPLIFY IT

After carrying out the second observation run, you are now in a much better position to decide whether to scrap your business or amplify its operations. Information is power and the second run has provided you with a lot of it.

Now, take some time and conduct some few types of analysis that will help you as an entrepreneur to choose a strategic way forward.

One of these analyses is the cost-benefit analysis. This type of analysis will enable you to know whether the cost of keeping your venture active is worth whatever benefit you derive from it.

You can also conduct a proper Monitoring and Evaluation (M&E) analysis. This will help you as an entrepreneur to always track the progress of your newly effected directives with ease. It will also help in ascertaining their effectiveness on various social as well as financial metrics.

Another analysis you can conduct is the SWOT analysis. This involves identifying all the Strengths, Weaknesses, Opportunities and Threats that your business faces. Knowing details about them will give you an edge as an entrepreneur in preventing crisis as well as avoiding decisions which may drive your business underground.

Another type of analysis you can conduct is the GAP analysis. This basically means looking at the earlier set objectives of the venture and listing down how many of them have been achieved so far and how many have not been achieved so far.

Apart from the above types of analysis, there are very many others that can be used in helping decide on the way forward like trend analysis.

The decision is entirely up to you as the entrepreneur.

Based on the budget you have, there is no limit as to the number of analysis you can conduct but just a point to remember; do not drown in them. There is a thing called over preparation and overthinking. Sometimes just do what is necessary and take a leap of faith on the rest especially where financial resources are limited.

Do not waste your time overspending in research and development when there is not much cash available for it. Remember to be prudent and to always seek the highest degree of profit maximization possible.

At this stage, you can also involve consultants provided that your budget allows it. They may be very much experienced in conducting the various types of analysis needed for your business. Apart from that, they will save you much valuable time that you would have otherwise dedicated elsewhere.

DEALS AND DOLLARS

Please note that this does not imply that you cannot do it yourself. Let me tell you that you can.

After performing all the necessary types of researches, it is now time to make one of the hardest decisions you might make as an entrepreneur. I t can only go two ways. You either scrap your business, which means closing down everything and liquidating everything or you can amplify it which means scaling up your operations.

What most people assume is that there is a third option which involves waiting. This waiting can be either for better results or enjoying what already is. Well, let me tell you today that the notion waiting is a third option is a blatant lie. There is no such thing as waiting just as Economists say that there is no such thing as a free lunch.

All the waiting process does is stagnate your business and drain you of all the cash available you have. Within no time at all you will find yourself in debt and lashing out on every entrepreneur you see walking in the street.

Sometimes in order to gain ground you need to walk backwards. If the business is not profitable, quit it and start another one as soon as possible. Things will never get better with a faulty business model. The sooner you realize this, the faster you can start another venture that may be successful.

If you decide to amplify it then be careful with your emotions and do not over amplify things. Some entrepreneurs end up as failures for making the mistake of growing their businesses too fast. It is important to be wise and execute events step by step. That is the only way that guarantees your business will not fail as a result of expanding too fast.

Always make sure that you not only breakeven but dominate the respective markets your business has ventured into before exploring other markets. Sometimes a step in the right direction and at the right pace wins the marathon.

The decision you make at this point greatly determines the future of your business. Be wise, prudent and cautious when deciding between whether to scrap it or to amplify it.

PART V: CONGRATULATIONS, NOW WHAT?

"NEVER, NEVER, NEVER GIVE UP."

-WINSTON CHURCHILL.

CHAPTER 1: CONCLUSION

You have made the ultimate decision of whether to scrap it or to amplify it. Just as consequences follow every other decision, there are consequences to this decision you have made.

If you decided to scrap it then you have to start all over again on a new venture. It will be hard especially emotionally for you as the entrepreneur but you will prevail. All you have to do is to follow the same process you did when embarking on the first journey of making your dreams a reality. Within no time at all, you will find yourself positioned strategically at a place where there is success left, right and centre. Through everything you will also learn new things and improve your business knowledge.

AUTHORED BY WILLIAM OCHIENG

In business there is never a loss to the entrepreneur because circumstances are either a blessing or a lesson. That is by definition what we call a win-win situation. All you need is patience and a lot of perseverance.

On the other hand, if you decided to amplify it then you still have the challenge of maintaining the momentum. Do not relax and lower your guard because I can tell you beyond any reasonable doubt that your competitors are not. Always invent and innovate new ways of doing things at your business and also new ways of keeping you customers satisfied, happy and interested in more.

Being an entrepreneur is more of a mindset than a job. Reason is that for jobs there is a time to go home where you are not required to think about work until the next day. For entrepreneurship, your mind must always be thinking business. It must always be looking for newer and better ways of doing things. The one moment that you stop thinking is the time you will be thrown out of business.

You need to constantly find ways of motivating yourself. Also seek advanced formal education most preferably in business studies. Go get a degree if you have to because your mind needs to be smarter and sharper than it was yesterday.

DEALS AND DOLLARS

In conclusion, I would like to wish you all the best as you venture out into the business world. Take all of my thoughts in this book and place them somewhere close to your heart. Also create room for your own ideas, inventions and innovations to my thoughts.

You are ready to start on the journey of creating a business that will change the world for good. A business that will have its name etched in history forever. All the guiding principles in this book serve to give your burning business desire a sense of direction. Follow them to the letter, seek more personalized advice from experts and success will be your portion.

Remember that there is no one in the world who can tell you how to run your business. You are your own boss. You set the standards and you have authority to raise the bar. Now the big question here is, are you ready, willing and able to be not only an entrepreneur but a successful human being? If so, then get down to business and start working on your dream.

You now have the ultimate license to build your dream.

Go do it.

THE END.

AUTHORED BY WILLIAM OCHIENG

ABOUT THE AUTHOR

William Omondi Ochieng is a Kenyan Author and Entrepreneur. He was born on 5th November 1997 in Nairobi City. Writing is his passion as well as part-time profession. From a young age, he has been obsessed by telling great stories. This unique interest led him to interacting with renowned story tellers on various writing projects while he was still studying in school.

William got his primary education at Busara Primary School located in Nairobi, Kenya. Upon completion of his studies, he was recognized by the Ministry of Education as the "Best male student in public primary". This led to him joining St. Thomas Aquinas High School which is also located in Nairobi Kenya. Upon completion of his studies there, he was recognized as "Student with the Spirit of Service" by the local authority. Apart from that, William was also able to scoop up other awards for being an active member in St. John Ambulance Service, earning a 1st degree black-belt in Karate, demonstrating outstanding student leadership qualities while serving as the medical captain in the school and being an active member in the Nairobi East Scouts Association (NESA).

Following the completion of his high school education, William was able to join the University of Nairobi (UON) and pursue a Bachelor of Arts (B.A) degree in Economics, Sociology and Philosophy.

Apart from this, he was also able to pursue the Certified Public Accountant (CPA) certification course and the Certified Investments and Financial Analyst (CIFA) certification course.

DEALS AND DOLLARS

William also earned certification in processing statutory deductions like NSSF, NHIF and all iTAX processes in Kenya as well as certification in various computerized accounting courses like QuickBooks, Sage, Pastel and Tally.

He is currently engaged in various entrepreneurial ventures. "Deals and Dollars" is his own authentic work developed for a period of three (3) years. During this time, William perfected the content and ensured that it met generally accepted international standards. The book is written using basic English and intended to serve as a learning, guiding and inspirational tool for all types of audience.

To contact William for any inquiries, thoughts, suggestions, business or just a chat, reach him directly through:

Email address: **williamochieng.author@gmail.com** or **williamochieng.business@gmail.com**

You can also follow him on:

Instagram:

www.instagram.com/mr.williamochieng or **@mr.williamochieng**

Twitter:

https://twitter.com/realLiamKings?s=09 or **@realLiamKings**

Facebook: **https://m.facebook.com/Liam.T.Kings?ref=bookmarks**

AUTHORED BY WILLIAM OCHIENG

NOTES

www.ingramcontent.com/pod-product-compliance
Lightning Source LLC
Chambersburg PA
CBHW070501220526
45466CB00004B/1912